Best wishes,

[illegible]

THE *Original* MEMORY ALBUM BOOK

SHEENA CABLE

NEW HOLLAND

To Tarli, my daughter, one of the bravest people I know

First published in 1998 by
New Holland Publishers (UK) Ltd
London • Cape Town • Sydney • Singapore

24 Nutford Place
London W1H 6DQ
United Kingdom

80 McKenzie Street
Cape Town 8001
South Africa

3/2 Aquatic Drive
Frenchs Forest, NSW 2086
Australia

ISBN 1 85368 989 0 (hb)
ISBN 1 85974 072 3 (pb)

Designed by: Grahame Dudley Associates
Photographer: Mark Tupper
Editorial direction: Coral Walker

Reproduction by cmyk Pre-press (Pty) Ltd
Printed and bound in Hong Kong
Produced by Sino Publishing House

Acknowledgements

The author and publishers would like to thank the following companies for their assistance in providing materials and equipment. Full details appear on pages 78–79.
First Class Stamps (everything for memory albums), Specialist Crafts (wide variety of craft products), Stone (blank albums p 16–17, photocorners, etc), Kodak (films and processing), Falkiner Fine Papers (suppliers of the marbled paper [Cockerell marbled paper K11T] shown on headings),
Greene & Stone (gilt wax), Cornelissen & Son (gold leaf).

From the author

As with all books there are many people who contribute to the finished article in many different ways, and this book is no exception. Firstly, I must thank Jane Lang who assists me, keeps my feet firmly on the ground and loves cutting, glueing, and generally playing with anything messy. Thank you Jane, I do appreciate it. Secondly, Coral Walker, who has given me lots of space, time, and understanding, when the going got tough. Thanks to Grahame Dudley, whose gentle nature and quiet disposition are infectious and his layout skills appreciated.
Thanks to Yvonne McFarlane who encouraged me to pursue this craft.
Thank you to my friend Helen Jarvis who put up with my children and my temperament.
Lastly, my family, my children Tarli, Jack and Madeleine who sometimes suffer for my art, and my long-suffering husband Richard, who never falters in his love and support.
To all my friends who willingly allowed me to pilfer their treasured photographs.

CONTENTS

INTRODUCTION

When I first heard about the exciting new craft of "memory albums", my initial reaction was "scrapbooks"! Old-fashioned scrapbooks, like the ones I had put together myself as a child. In a way, I was right, but as I began to spend time studying this craft, I realized that this is not just something for children to do, but an opportunity for everyone to turn today's events into the treasured memories of tomorrow.

My mother-in-law still has many albums of photographs from when she lived in Canada, while her children were growing up. She loves looking through the albums – and so do her children and grandchildren – but, sadly, many of the dates, names and other clues to bring the pictures to life, have long been forgotten.

To stop this happening with the memories from my own family's life, I am putting together albums celebrating not just the momentous occasions – weddings, graduations, new babies – but also the fun times (vacations and holidays, children's parties, a weekend away) and brief moments (a New Year's party, special dinner or a friend's visit). I'm including all the memorabilia as well as the photographs to make a personal library for us, that I hope future generations will also treasure.

But memory albums are more than just a collection of family snapshots and ephemera. Each album is like a handcrafted book – it is designed, illustrated, decorated and embellished using any number of craft techniques so that, once you begin, you will have difficulty knowing where to stop.

Everyone's favourite papercraft pleasures are here, from stamping, calligraphy and stencilling, to painting, papermaking and decorative punching. And there's more: using die cuts and templates, creating decorative edges,

mounts and borders, embellishing with paint, fabric, embroidery, stickers. You can even make and bind your own album from scratch. The design features you choose are only limited by your imagination.

This book is full of useful ideas and tips for creating your very own memory albums. Memory-making in our house involves the whole family: selecting the photographs and other memorabilia, deciding how to display them, cropping and sticking the selected pictures into the album. We spend many hours working together, talking as we cut and stick, about our shared memories held in each of the photographs.

I hope you have as much fun making memories as my family have with ours.

Sheena Cable

PHOTOGRAPHS

Photography is one of the world's most popular hobbies. As the price of cameras has dropped, so the hobby has grown, and now very few homes are without a camera of some description. Even if you forget to take your camera, you can pick up a disposable one, so there is never an excuse for not snapping those happy and memorable occasions.

TAKING PICTURES

Having a camera is one thing. Knowing how to use it to get the best results possible is quite another. On these pages we give you some hints and tips to improve your photographic skills.

There are two keys to successful photography and even if you only snap with a disposable camera they still apply. Firstly, composition: think about the subject of your photograph. Look through your viewfinder and check if there are any unwanted items in your shot that can be avoided or removed: telegraph posts, scaffolding, an unsightly mess on a food table. Moving objects, cars and people can also be distractions. Think about repositioning your subject or waiting until the moving object has passed.

The second key is light: when to use a flash indoors, and working with the sunlight – instead of against it – outdoors.

To avoid red-eye, especially if you are using a camera with a built-in flash, it may be helpful to get the subject to look at a light before taking your picture. This will cause the iris to become smaller therefore the light has less chance to reach the retina and bounce back. If you are using a camera with a detached flash, try bouncing the flash off a white or light coloured ceiling.

NOT SO GOOD The subject is facing into the sun which causes her to squint. See also how the strong light full on her face "bleaches out" her features.

MUCH BETTER By asking the subject to turn slightly away, she can smile without squinting. Her features are also given much more definition.

DURING THE COURSE OF THE DAY The same scene can look quite different depending on the time of day you choose to shoot. Left: mid morning. The sky is blue and the sun is reaching its zenith. A perfect holiday picture.

BY MID AFTERNOON The light has changed considerably and the shadows begin to lengthen. The weather is also cloudier.

EARLY EVENING The headland begins to disappear in the evening light. The shadows are now much heavier and the tide well out.

If you are working with older photographs and the subjects already have red-eye, then the use of a red-eye pen sorts the problem out.

Outside, natural light is ever changing as the day moves from early morning to evening. If you are photographing a static object, both the colour and the shadow will change throughout the day (see page 9). Depending on your project, you may want to take a number of shots at different times of the day and then decide which one looks the best. However, if your subject is movable, you can position it in a spot where the light is better. Check the direction and glare of the sun and, if you are photographing a person, avoid the subject looking straight into it as this will cause squinting.

QUICK TIPS FOR BETTER PHOTOGRAPHS

- Keep yourself and your camera steady. Lean on something to support your arms if it helps.
- For parties, weddings and other celebrations: vary the viewpoint by shooting the activity from different levels. Try standing on a chair, or even lying on the ground to get an interesting vantage point.
- Photograph babies in soft light. Get down on their level before shooting.
- For birthday candle shots use a fast film (ISO 400 or above) and avoid using a flash.
- Shoot quickly and take several shots of the same event/people to ensure one good result.
- If you can, put people in bright clothes or carrying bright objects to the centre of the shot; on the finished photograph it will help concentrate the viewer's eye and provide a good composition.
- Races on sports days are always best shot from the finishing line, facing the participants.
- Insufficient light or long distance means that presentation ceremonies, such as graduations, are difficult to photograph. Instead, capture the event by taking shots of the key people outside as soon as you can.
- Arrange people close together: gaps are exaggerated by the camera.
- On holidays, take shots of the beach from higher up, if you can. This provides a far more interesting picture and shows the varying colours of the water and the contour of the land.
- If you want to include someone in a holiday landscape, do not put them in middle distance. Instead, place them to one side or bring them closer to the camera and have them in profile, looking at the scene beyond.
- Try to capture typical sightseeing shots in the early morning or evening to avoid the inevitable crowds.
- When shooting snow, bear in mind that your camera's auto-exposure system may get confused and under-expose your shot. For the serious photographer – use fill-in flash to compensate.

CARE AND RESTORATION

To last well, photographs – whether old or new – require a little tender loving care. Storing photographs in an album means using the right materials to prevent their deterioration.

The chemicals (namely silver) in photographs taken in the first part of this century have proved to be remarkably stable and many pictures from that time are still sharp and clear with all their original features intact. Unfortunately, more modern snaps – those taken in the late 1960s, for example, are unlikely to fare so well, as you may have already discovered. However, whatever the date of your photographs, you can preserve them by observing a few simple rules.

High humidity speeds up a chemical reaction on photographs which leads to their fading and discoloration. Temperature control is therefore essential. With every 18°C rise in temperature the deterioration level doubles for your photographs, so try to keep your pictures in a dry environment. Fluctuations in temperature are also harmful and for this reason it is better to store your photographs in a spare room wardrobe or drawer rather than in the attic.

Light causes fading and yellowing, so keep your photographs away from direct sunlight.

Finally, certain storage materials can react to photographic materials which may cause damage over time: acidic ground wood pulp sleeves, rubber bands and low quality adhesives can all cause damage. Select acid-free products to protect your pictures from humidity and to prevent any adverse chemical reaction.

RESTORATION OF OLD PHOTOGRAPHS

Many reputable photographic processors are now able to restore and reproduce old photographs at a reasonable cost. For your memory album this service is ideal, especially if the original pictures are stained or torn. Look in Yellow Pages or contact a local photographic bureau for more information.

MODERN TECHNOLOGY means that old photographs can now be "cleaned up" and made fit for display.

CROPPING & MOUNTING

Cropping and mounting your pictures creates a far more interesting and dynamic page in your album and also helps solve problems of badly composed photographs.

As we have seen, many snaps are taken with little thought given to the background, which could be messy or unattractive. Cropping your photograph involves cutting it in order to edit the composition, or as a decorative feature. Cropping is the answer to many a problem, and you will be amazed at the results that this can create.

Look at the example that I have shown. The photograph is very typical, showing a rather uninspiring background as well as a large wastebin. By taking a craft knife and cutting around the main character you instantly lose all the items that spoil your photograph.

Cropping can be used as little or as dramatically as you like. For example, you could draw a square or rectangle around the main image on the photograph and cut out most of the background (which may contain items that detract from the central subject). This is generally what happens to photographs shot for magazines or newspapers, after all. Alternatively, you could cut out all of the background, by cutting – very carefully – around the image.

Of course, you may only wish to crop the corners to shape it and to add a little definition. Decorative punches are good for this.

CHOP CHOP! Even by cutting away most of the background (bottom left) the picture is improved. Try decorative-edged scissors for a deckle effect. Close cropping (top) creates even more impact.

MOUNTING

To enhance your photograph further, why not mount it.

A mount is usually made from one or more pieces of decorative paper. A simple method is to cut a mount in the same shape as your cropped photograph but slightly larger, so that the mount "frames" the picture. Choose a colour that will complement your photograph, something that will tone with the clothing the subject is wearing or colours that tie in with the theme of your album.

Try tearing the edge of handmade papers to create a folk art look, and applying this mount on top of another, similar paper.

Apart from a square or circle, there are many fun, shaped templates available, and these also could be tied in with the theme of your pages or album. A cake template, for example, is ideal for a birthday party picture or a jack-o-lantern for spooky Halloween photographs.

FRAMED A little frame has been made from thin, gold-coloured moulding to fit snugly around the photograph. The whole thing is then mounted on to a piece of Japanese paper that has been gently torn for an interesting effect.

ALBUMS

There are plenty of blank albums on the market from which to choose, or you can make your own from just a few simple materials. Whatever your taste, subject or budget, the next few pages offer suggestions, instructions and advice for buying, making and personalizing your very own memory album.

CHOOSING YOUR ALBUM

With such a wide choice of blank albums available, you should have little problem buying one suitable for your chosen project. Why not decorate the cover to coordinate with the theme inside?

Traditional photograph albums are probably the most commonly available types and these can be bought at a wide variety of outlets. The pages inside should be acid-free and the album or its packaging should have a label indicating this.

These albums come in a variety of bindings: rigid, spiral bound or ring binders with transparent pockets for holding the photographs. Obviously the latter is of little use to the scrapbooker, but the first two types can be personalized (see pages 20–27) and transformed into a unique memory album.

For the enthusiast, specialist blank memory albums are available, the most economical and popular being the simple three-ring binder. These contain polypropylene

PHOTO ALBUMS By customizing the covers of traditional photograph albums (see pages 20-27) you can transform them into your own personal memory books.

wallets to safeguard your album pages and are an excellent choice if you are working on an on-going project, for example, a childhood album. Pages can be added as time progresses, the only limitation being the size of the binder.

Specialist loose leaf albums are one of the most expensive of the albums available, with covers that you can decorate yourself and the facility to add extra pages whenever necessary.

Whatever your decision, the following pages show how easy it is to customize any album to make each one an individual work of art.

For the more ambitious, why not try making your own album from scratch. Full instructions appear overleaf.

ALBUM CHOICE Spiral-bound albums like these are becoming more common and look great with just a small decoration stuck to the cover to personalize them. They come in a range of sizes and are available from a wide selection of stockists. More details appear on page 78.

MAKING YOUR OWN ALBUM

A simple, hand-made memory album is not difficult to make and would be a wonderful gift. What about a "grandchild" album specially for the grandparents.

One of the most appealing things about making memory albums is the extent to which you can stretch your creativity to any number of different crafts.

This album is made from easy-to-find materials, is neat and compact and is ideal for a "mini memory" such as a weekend holiday or an anniversary party.

If you wish to make an album like this you will need the following :

1. *Glue the stiff cardboard to the wrong side of the larger piece of fabric, leaving a border of approximately 3 cm (1⅛ in) all around the outside of the cardboard and a gap of 1.5 cm (½ in) between the centre of the cardboard pieces. Fold down the overlap neatly, mitring the corners to keep the fabric flat.*

- 2 pieces of stiff cardboard (A5 size)
- 2 pieces of covering material (fabric or paper) one measuring about 44 x 28 cm (17¼ x 11 in), one measuring 19 x 30 cm (7½ x 11¾ in)
- 4 pieces of paper/lightweight card (A4 size folded in half)
- fabric glue
- gold cord
- 2 gold tassels

BOOKBINDING

Making your own album from scratch is extremely satisfying and, you never know, you might end up enjoying bookbinding as a hobby in its own right. Start small, as this little album here, and you can always move on to making more sophisticated albums with stitched or bolted bindings. Many craft shops stock binding materials and there are various books which tackle the subject in more detail.

2. *Glue the second piece of fabric onto the inside of the album cover. Smooth the fabric flat and make sure there are no creases or bubbles. Leave to dry.*

3. *It is probably easier to decorate your pages before adding them to the cover, but there is no reason why you cannot do this afterwards. Tie the pages into the cover using the gold cord. Finish off by tying the tassels to the ends of the cord.*

NOSTALGIA This small hand-made album forms a miniature family history.

PERSONALIZING YOUR COVER

Spend a little time customizing the cover of your album – it is not difficult, great fun and will provide the finishing touch to the memories within.

On the following pages, we have decorated various types of albums in a number of ways. Use these ideas to inspire you to customize your own covers.

STARS AND HEARTS

You will need:
decorative fabric to wrap around your album with sufficient overlap allowance
plain fabric to cover inside back and front
fabric glue
cord
small satin heart

1. *Open your album, lying it on top of the decorative fabric and cut all the way round, allowing at least 2.5 cm (1 in) to turn inside.*

2. *Spread the album back, front and spine with glue and carefully wrap the decorative fabric around it, smoothing it into place. Keep the fabric taut and turn in the excess neatly to the inside.*

3. *Cut the plain fabric to fit the inside front and back of the cover. Spread glue over the album and stick one piece of fabric on the inside front, and the other on the inside back to give a neat finish.*

4. *Lay the cord down the middle of the album and tie in place at the bottom. To finish, stick the heart in place on the centre of the cover.*

ALL HEART The perfect place to store love letters and romantic memorabilia.

WILD ANIMALS

You will need:

animal print fabric to cover back and front of album with no overlap
gold foil paper
small wooden animal (old piece of jewellery or small ornament)
black paper
glue
strong glue or glue gun

1. *Cut the animal print fabric into two pieces, making sure they fit the front and back covers exactly. Glue the back cover fabric in place.*

2. *For the front cover, fold the fabric in half and cut out a pointed oval shape on the fold which will become the shield when unfolded.*

3. *Stick the gold foil on the front of the album. You will need just enough to create the shield shape when the fur fabric is placed over the top.*

4. *Glue the fabric on to the front cover, so that the shield is now apparent. Cut six thin strips from the black paper and glue in place on the gold foil to complete the shield.*

5. *Finally, using the strong glue, stick the wooden animal on top in the centre.*

JUNGLE FUN Fur fabrics make great covers as they don't fray. Look for scraps in the remnants basket, as you will only need a small amount.

Feather and Bead

You will need:

brown parcel-wrapping paper
small sheet of leafy handmade paper
small piece of brown corrugated paper
brown feather
assorted wooden and small glass beads
small shell
glue gun and glue sticks

1. *Wrap the cover of the album in the brown wrapping paper using the matt side of the paper as the right side (face up). Stick in place, taking care the glue does not show.*

2. *Depending upon the size of your album, cut a rectangle out of the handmade paper (this album measured roughly 31 x 30 cm [12½ x 12 in] and the rectangle of handmade paper was cut to 21 x 17 cm [8¼ x 6¾ in]). Stick this to the centre of the front of the album as shown.*

3. *Cut a 10 cm (4 in) square out of the corrugated paper and stick this on top of the rectangle.*

4. *Using a glue gun or glue stick, stick the feather firmly in place on the corrugated paper. Add the beads and shell on top of the feather, glueing them down to create a pleasing arrangement. (The beads could be placed so that an initial or symbol is depicted.)*

NOTICEBOARD

You will need:
coloured card for the front of the album
3 m (3 yd) of 7 mm (¼ in) wide ribbon/tape
gold coloured paper fasteners
glue and sticky tape

1. *Measure the front of your album and cut the coloured card to fit exactly.*

2. *Taking the ribbon/tape, stretch it from one corner to the other and fasten to the back of the card with sticky tape. The tape needs to be taut, but not so tight that the cardboard bends.*

3. *Stretch the next piece of ribbon/tape from the opposite corners so the pieces cross in the middle. Continue stretching and securing on the back at regular intervals.*

4. *Using the paper fasteners secure the ribbon/tape at alternate points as shown.*

5. *Finally stick the cardboard to the front of the album. Slot the photographs and memorabilia behind the ribbon and stick in place.*

WOODEN ALBUM

You will need:

wooden album cover (see suppliers on page 78)
primer
parchment-coloured matt emulsion paint
base and top coats of crackle glaze varnish
raw sienna oil paint
paintbrushes
coloured, textured paste (optional)

1. *Paint the outside of the album with the primer and allow to dry. Apply two coats of emulsion paint, allowing each one to dry thoroughly between coats.*

2. *Using a paintbrush, paint on the base coat of crackle glaze and allow it to dry. Next, paint on the top coat of crackle glaze and allow the wood to dry overnight. Fine cracks will now have appeared over the surface of the album.*

3. *With a paper towel, rub the raw sienna paint into the cracks. Leave to dry for 24 hours. Rub off the excess oil paint with a damp cloth. Seal the whole cover with acrylic varnish.*

4. *To finish, I have relief-stencilled a pear tree using some coloured, textured paste. (For suppliers of a range of stencils and stencil paints, see suppliers on page 78.)*

BABY COVER

You will need:

4 pastel-coloured glass nuggets
tracing paper and pencil
white backing card
cloud template (see page 43)
pale blue ink pad and small sponge
two pieces of backing paper in contrasting designs and toning colours
glue
tube of fabric paint in a metallic colour

1. *Make a template of the front cover of your album using the tracing paper and pencil. Transfer this onto the white backing card (make two if you wish to cover the back of your album). Cut the card to shape.*

2. *Using the cloud template and the pale blue inkpad, work the cloud design with the sponge on to the backing card. Only use a very small amount of ink on the sponge to achieve a subtle effect.*

3. *When dry, cut a rectangular shape out of one of the backing sheets and the pram shape out of the other (trace the templates shown here if you wish). Cut the shapes out and glue them into position on to the cloud covered card.*

4. *Take the fabric paint and pipe around the pram shape, drawing in the wheels and handle as you go. Work the same around the rectangle. Allow to dry overnight.*

5. *Finally, stick the glass nuggets in the corners and glue the whole thing on to the album.*

BABY BLUES
You can create a traditional blue or pink baby album, or choose lemon or mint green as optional pastels.

Fabric Cover

You will need:
chosen fabric 137 x 34 cm (54 x 13½ in)
bonding web
open weave fabric 10 cm (4 in) square
wadding 8 cm (3 in) square
gold thread and invisible thread
gold braid and small brass charms

1. *Turn the fabric under 1 cm (½ in) on the shortest side and secure with bonding web.*

2. *Place the fabric right side up. Bring in the outer edges by 33 cm (13 in), leaving a 2 cm (¾ in) gap.*

3. *Machine stitch the front and back together with a 1 cm (½ in) seam allowance.*

4. *Turn right side out and insert your album. Mark the centre of the front. Remove the album.*

5. *Lay the wadding on the centre mark with the open weave fabric over the top. Pin around the wadding and backstitch with gold thread around the pin line, securing the wadding and leaving a 1 cm (½ in) raw edge. Fray the edge up to the stitching.*

6. *Make a bow from the braid and secure on the fabric square with invisible thread. Stitch on the charms with invisible thread.*

TARTAN COVER

You will need:

tartan fabric to cover complete album allowing for at least 2.5 cm (1 in) overlap
fabric glue
plain fabric to cover inside front and back
old frame or scraps of gilded moulding
strong glue
small freehand painting

1. *Cover the album with the fabrics, following steps 1 - 3 on page 20 (Stars and Hearts Album).*

2. *Stick the freehand painting in the centre of the cover and enclose with the frame or gilded moulding.*

TRADITIONAL TOUCH Scottish roots? Then this cover is perfect for a family tree or history. Or use the same concept for a Christmas album, perhaps with a seasonal picture.

DECORATION

Once you have your photos, memorabilia and album - where do you start? There are so many ways to decorate your new memory album. On the next few pages, I explain and explore some of the most popular techniques and crafts that you can employ to make the pages of your memory album so very special. Try stamping, sponging and adding stickers to the pages, use fabric and embroidery, parchment craft, embellished hand-writing and much more.

SPECIALIST PAPERS

Paper has become an art form in itself, with a wide range of beautiful writing and decorative papers now available. Special papers add flair and individuality to your album.

There are some exquisite papers now available to buy that will really enhance the pages of your albums. Often sold as gift wrap, you can also buy handmade papers in writing paper-sized sheets. In craft shops you can probably buy these papers in small packets. They are perfect for mounting on to a plain backing sheet (acid-free, of course) and can provide decoration to your page.

If you want to add a very personal touch, and have fun in the process, then why not make some paper yourself? By adding acid-free inks and experimenting with other materials, the results can be stunning. Different effects can also be introduced to the paper after it has been made.

PAPER PARADISE Fabulous coloured papers (above) look great as decorative strips running down the edge of your page, or as a background to a Christmas memory. Plainer papers in neutral shades look beautiful as pages themselves. Try utilizing them in a handmade album.

MAKING YOUR OWN PAPER

For beginners to papermaking, it may be best to start with a papermaking kit. These are available from good art and craft suppliers (see pages 78–79). The kits usually include paper pulp, aquapel size (which is added to the pulping process to produce stronger paper that is resistant to water-based colour medium), a papermaking frame and gauze and a paper press.

Most of this equipment could be used a number of times and the small expense will allow you to make good quality and attractive papers.

Once you have learned the basics of making paper, you can add extra ingredients such as flower petals, glitter, silk threads or coloured inks to add interest and variety to your papers.

PAPER CHOICE Seek out specialist suppliers who will be able to offer a variety of handmade papers. Look for thick, fibrous papers which make good album covers as well as flimsy Japanese paper (pink, above), which is gossamer-fine yet remarkably strong and perfect for whimsical decoration.

HOMEMADE These homemade papers (above) were made with a simple papermaking kit. Making your own paper, rather than buying it, means that you are not limited to the colours and styles held by stockists. You can make papers to fit your own colour scheme or theme.

STAMPING

Rubber stamps are ideal for using in a memory album. They are simple to operate and there is such a wide range available to buy that you can be sure of finding appropriate stamps for almost any subject. Most stamping inks are water-based and acid free, so they will not stain your clothes.

You can use your stamps with a colour brush pen or a stamp pad. For a vibrant, primary effect, use colour brush pens only. For a subtle look, colour the stamp using a colour brush pen, then infill the stamped design with watercolour pens. For an even more subtle effect, mix the ink from your pads with a little water on a palette.

You can stamp directly on your album page or you can stamp onto a separate piece of paper. When it is dry, cut out the stamp using a craft knife, then stick it carefully in place. Of course, you can also make stamps from vegetables, corks or sponges.

THIS TRAVEL STAMP IS PERFECT FOR A HOLIDAY MEMORY ALBUM.

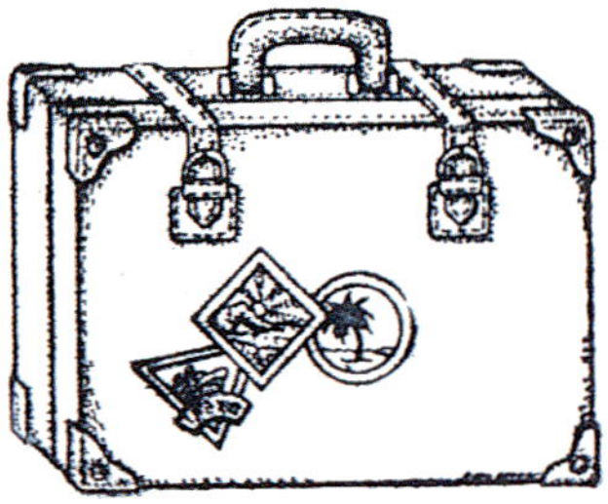

1. *Using a clean rubber stamp, colour brush the raised area of the stamp, making sure all of it is covered. Work quickly as the inks dry quite fast. Press the stamp down carefully onto your paper or card, then lift.*

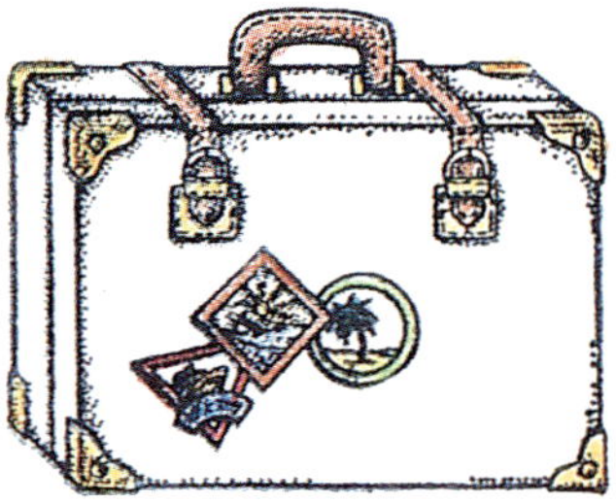

2. *Colour in the smaller areas of the design first, adding shading for a more three-dimensional look.*

3. *Colour in the larger areas evenly and add more shading if you can.*

STAMPING MOUNTS

Stamp a mount around a picture in your memory album for a really gorgeous effect. There is a wide range of stamping mounts available and by choosing your own colours and colouring technique you can adapt them to suit the picture.

The appropriate mount will also enhance the picture or photograph.

The ornate and decorative stamps shown here complement the old black and white photographs. Try modern frames for contemporary pictures. Several companies provide illustrated brochures showing the full range of stamps available; see page 79 for more information.

FANCY FRAMES These ornate frames work well with old black and white photographs, but there are plenty of modern-style stamps to choose from.

HAND TINTING For more decorative mounts you will need to stamp onto some scrap paper first (above). Colour the stamp in then carefully cut it out with a knife. Stick the photograph onto some mounting paper or directly on the album page then position the stamped mount over the top to frame the picture (right).

PUNCHES SCISSORS STICKERS & DIE CUTS

For anyone new to memory albums, you might be delighted to discover the array of tools and materials specifically designed to help decorate your page.

Anyone keen on this hobby is probably a stationery lover. Paper, pens, stickers and shapes will appeal to you as they do to me. I love rummaging through all this paraphernalia as it inspires me to decorate my memory albums in different ways and using a multitude of things.

The manufacturers have met the demand of hobbyists by producing a whole range of tools and materials to add that something special to the scrapbook page.

The little decorative **punches** are one of my favourites. Not only do I use the punch to decorate the page but I also use the shapes or "confetti" produced by the punch. A good tip is to keep the shapes in envelopes so that you can use them for an up-and-coming project.

The wonderful fancy edged **scissors** are very versatile: use these to cut out your mounts, photographs or simply to edge your page.

Die cuts are simply shapes, words or numbers cut from coloured paper. They can be bought in almost any shape that you might want. Now, you can also produce them from CD discs designed to work in your PC.

You can use your die cuts in a number of ways, for example, to mount your photograph, to create a backdrop to your work, or as a large number indicating a birthday or anniversary.

Stickers are readily available,

DECORATIVE EDGING
Punches can clip into the borders of mounts, the edges of photos themselves as well as providing "confetti" shapes which you can use elsewhere.

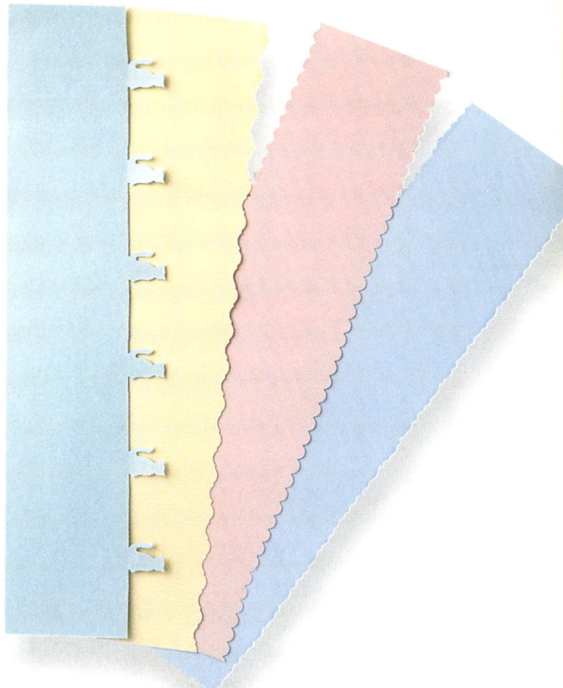

covering almost every topic imaginable, from snappy children's shapes, such as teddy bears or clowns, to beautiful Victorian facsimiles of people, flowers or fairies.

Most stickers are self adhesive and are peeled easily from a backing sheet. Alternatively, pre-gummed shapes are available in small bags. These need moistening like postage stamps.

For a list of stockists who will be able to supply you with a brochure or catalogue, see page 79.

DECORATION CRAZY Fancy edged scissors provide different cut edges to your pages, mounts, photographs or pieces of decorative paper used in your memory album (above), while die cuts can provide letters, words and interesting shapes (above left). You'll have fun choosing from the enormous selection of stickers currently on the market (below).

TEMPLATES & STENCILS

Wonderful, time-saving items: stencils and templates are essential tools in a scrapbooker's workcase.

TEMPLATES

A template is the opposite of a stencil, being something around which you draw to create a shape or image. Usually made from rigid plastic, templates are invaluable for cutting out both your photographs and mounts to shape. When using a template, cut with a craft knife to create a clean, sharp edge.

You can also make a template from an existing item, for example, if you want to create a large circular shape you can draw around a small plate. It sounds elementary, but don't forget to improvise when designing your pages.

STENCILS AND STENCILLING

Stencilling, generally, has become a very popular decorative effect over recent years. And, of course, it is not something that is limited to walls or furniture. Small stencils – perfect for memory albums – can be bought to add embellishment to your pages. The beauty of a stencil is the speed with which you can add decoration, and the fact that a repeat design can be applied which looks professional and artistic.

The most popular stencils available in stationery outlets are usually alphabets, with upper and lower case letters and various pieces of punctuation, such as exclamation or question marks.

These are useful for adding headings to your page and are a great boon if your handwriting is poor.

Picture or border stencils are also available, but if you have trouble finding a pattern or image, you can always make your own stencil.

SHAPELY SHAPES Templates are useful for scribing neat and accurate shapes, especially for photographs and mounts, as the top picture demonstrates.

TO MAKE YOUR OWN STENCIL

Stencils are easy enough to make from a drawing, tracing or photocopy. The key to success is to keep the design simple.

You can either draw your design freehand or copy something from a magazine or postcard. Whichever you choose, you must make sure the final design is the size you want – and for a memory album it will need to be quite small to fit on the pages. A photocopier will reduce any given design.

You will need

Oiled stencil card or clear acetate
pencil
permanent marker pen
cutting mat
sharp craft knife

1. *Transfer your design on to the acetate or card. As acetate is clear, you can simply place your design underneath and draw on the acetate with permanent marker. For stencil card, use carbon paper between the design and card, pressing hard on the lines of the drawing. Of course, you can draw the design freehand directly on to the card.*

2. *Use a sharp craft knife and score out the design, always pulling the blade towards you and turning the stencil as you work (see left).*

If you make any mistakes, use masking or sticky tape to patch up the card.

Stencils can be used over and over again. Sponge them clean between use and when they are dry keep them stored flat.

HANDWRITING & DIARIES

The text that accompanies your photographs is almost as important as the pictures themselves. Don't worry if you're not sure what or how to write – here we give you some tips.

If you are not happy with your handwriting, consider this. When have you happened upon some handwriting of your grandmother's or some other past relative, and not loved what you saw? It is such a personal treasure. No matter what your handwriting is like, I can assure you that your family for generations to come will treasure every bit of it. Your handwriting will become a memento of the person you were.

One of the saddest things while looking through old photograph albums is that no one can remember who is in the pictures, where they were taken, or when they were taken.

To avoid this happening with your albums, there are four "W"s to remember. Who is in the photograph, where were they at the time of the photograph, what were they doing and when was the photograph taken.

You may like to write a little more text, perhaps some witty

BEAUTIFUL SCRIPT Illuminated lettering is an ancient art worth studying for ideas for your own memory albums. You will need to use a fine graphic drawing pen.

STYLISH LETTERS Practise lettering to achieve a neat hand. The examples shown here are written with a calligraphy or italic nib which creates both a thick and thin line. Several of the pens specifically manufactured for memory albums can produce handwriting like this.

comments about each photograph. If the memory is about an exotic holiday or a childhood event you may even wish to write a whole page of text. You may write a diary during your holiday which you wish to include with the photographs in the finished memory album. Each photograph could relate to a certain part of your text. A childhood event could be the day your son became a cub scout. Here, you might like to include the cub scout promise in the text.

HANDWRITING AND LETTERING

If you really do feel that your lettering could do with a bit of a brush up, then trace the basic alphabet and practise writing the letters out using guidelines to achieve regular and even writing. Titling your pages always benefits from a little extra special effort, so consider using decorative handwriting for this.

To alter the look of the basic letters there are a number of simple things you could do. Add a dot to the open ends of the letters. Add a straight short line to the ends of the letters. Try making the capital letter at the beginning of each phrase or paragraph rather special.

Try some puff lettering. Start by writing the letters individually then re-write the word with the letters slightly behind each other. At this point add small lines around the inside of the letters to turn them into "quilted" lettering. You really can let your imagination run wild.

PENS

There is an excellent array of pens for use in memory albums, with colours abounding and different nibs for various effects.

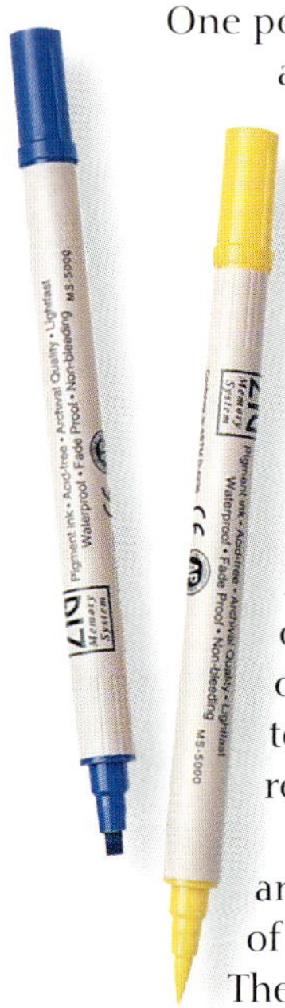

One popular pen in the memory album circuit is the gel ink pen. This pen is available in a vast selection of colours and has a wonderfully smooth writing action.

If you want a pen with a difference, why not try the brush-and-scroll pens? One end of the pen has a brush, which is great for colouring in large letters. The other end is double tipped which writes in double image. Take a little time to practise with this pen – it really is fun.

Traditional calligraphy pens are ink pens with a selection of italic nibs and coloured inks. These produce beautiful lettering but do need some practice to get a full range of effects. The colourful Zig calligraphy pens are an alternative which I think are really worth investing in. Each pen is double-ended, with a thick and thin end and, again, with a little time and experience you can achieve quite remarkable results.

It is important to check before you buy any pens or crayons that they are acid-free, achival quality. The acids and chemicals contained in some inks could have a disastrous effect on your photographs.

CALLIGRAPHY

The word "calligraphy" – quite literally – means beautiful writing. It has become an ancient art because mechanized printing and, more recently, the personal computer or word processor, have diminished the need to write with style and care. For your memory album you can, of course, print out captions to your photographs and ephemera from your computer, but how much more artistic and rewarding to try some beautiful writing yourself.

In order to turn lettering into calligraphy, some study has to be made into the basic forms of letters, how they are worked and placed onto the page.

The tools for calligraphy are few and relatively cheap. Paper, pencil, ruler, followed by inks, and penholder with nibs or italic writing pens.

There are many good books available on the subject, and for the traditional alphabets it is worth borrowing or buying a copy to work from.

Start by tracing the alphabets shown to establish a confident hand. Hold your pen comfortably and then practise the strokes "freehand". The more you practise, the more confident you will become. If you are nervous writing straight into your album, write first on some beautiful paper then cut this out and stick it in place on the page.

OTHER DECORATIVE EFFECTS

There are so many other decorative effects that you can use in your memory albums. In this section you will find some of my favourites, but remember this is your album, your ideas, your memories!

EMBROIDERY

Being a silk ribbon embroiderer, and in fact a lover of all embroidery, I like to include some of my work either inside or on the cover of my albums. Try to work embroidery that enhances your project. If you are working embroidery for the cover of your album, remember to make some preparation for storage so that the stitching will not spoil.

Another way to use embroidery is to mount your photographs. The piece of work shown below is stitched onto moiré silk using embroidery silks, silk and satin ribbon. It is a charming touch to add providing you have plenty of time to work it in.

Any scrap of embroidery can lift a page.

For those keen on cross-stitch, the mini-kits available from sewing and craft shops can make ideal decorations for your page. Alternatively, embroider an initial or small motif on to a small piece of linen as a way of personalizing your album.

PRESSED FLOWERS

Another beautiful way to enhance those memories, pressed flowers have been decorating books and cards for decades. Flowers from a bride's bouquet or from somewhere you have visited make excellent specimens. Flowers that you have been given for a special reason are also worth preserving. It is important to press your flowers very carefully to ensure that they are completely dry before you mount them into your memory album.

MAKING A SIMPLE FLOWER PRESS

Simple blooms press more easily than multi-petalled flowers; the latter need separating before you can press them successfully.

Lay your flowers on to blotting paper, leaving sufficient space around each one. Lay more blotting paper on top. Now place the blotting paper on to a piece of corrugated cardboard and place another piece of cardboard on top. This cardboard "sandwich" should now be placed in between two heavy books, making sure the books completely overlap all the edges of the cardboard.

Every two to four days place another heavy book on top. Check after ten days. The flowers should take between ten days and three weeks to dry completely, ready for use.

FEMININE TOUCH Beautiful cross stitch embroidery (top) makes a wonderful addition to the memory album page. Or add pressed flowers – a simple, inexpensive and exquisite decoration. So, salvage the bridesmaid's posy or gather a few blooms while on holiday to press and include in your album later.

SPONGING

Sometimes sponging a backing page can look really effective. You can use acid-free ink or watercolour paint to sponge your design. Allow the page to dry before you start to work on it.

A light cloud effect can look especially attractive. I tend to use my rubber stamp ink pad to work a cloud-sponged page, as the effect is more delicate. You will need a cloud template or rather, make your own by cutting the shape from some cardboard. A small piece of natural sponge and a light blue ink pad are the only other requirements.

Start at the top of the page and position the template. Using a very dry sponge and only a little ink sponge down the page moving the template into different positions.

SPONGE CRAZY Bold effects can be worked with paints (above). Ink pads create a more subtle impression (below).

MARBLING

A marbled effect on paper or fabric has a timeless quality and is one of the many craft projects to consider including in your memory albums.

Traditionally, marbling was used to edge the pages of accounts ledgers – the idea being that should pages be removed, then this could be detected by the break in the pattern!

There are various types of marbling, but the principles are more or less the same. The technique involves floating inks or paints onto the surface of water or size. These colours are swirled or stirred to create a pattern. The design is then transferred onto paper or fabric.

For memory albums, marbling can be used for backing a page, on the inside of the covers – as in many traditional books – or on the front of your album cover.

You will need:

large plastic container not used for food, perhaps an old ice-cream tub
water
oil-based colour
paper
wooden lollypop stick

1. *Fill the tub with water.*

2. *Drop the oil-based colour into the water; you may want to add two or three toning or contrasting colours.*

3. *Swirl the water around with the lollypop stick.*

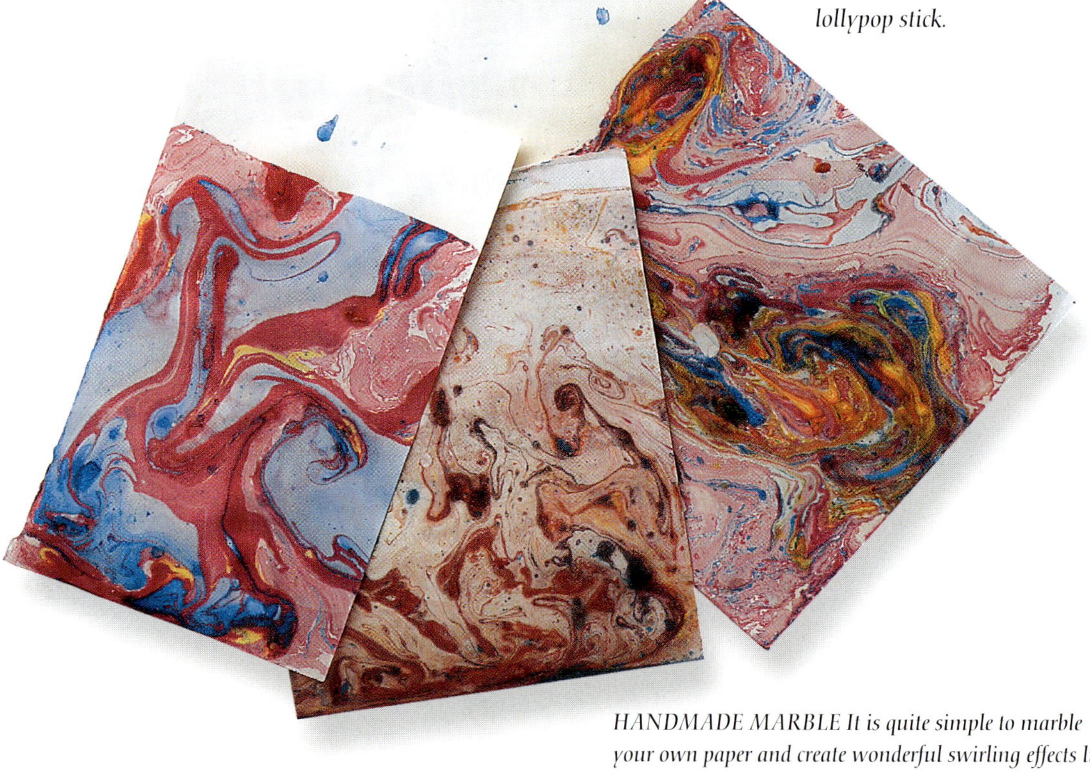

HANDMADE MARBLE It is quite simple to marble your own paper and create wonderful swirling effects like those shown here. Even if you are not happy with the whole piece, you can cut out part of the paper to use.

BRAIDS AND TRIMS Fabric samples, braids and cords all make useful additions. Use wide ribbon as a marker, for example, by running it down the centre of the album.

4. *Place your paper gently onto the surface of the water then lift it very carefully out again. Your paper should be marbled.*

5. *Allow the paper to dry naturally – you do not want your paper to curl and ripple.*

FREEHAND PAINTING

If you are a whizz with a paintbrush, then why not decorate your pages with some of your own artwork. If done well, this can be magnificent, but try not to let the artwork take over, allow it to enhance your album.

KIDS' STUFF Children love to be involved in memory-making and will be thrilled to offer their talents to the unfolding pages. Their paintings, say, of Daddy or where they went on holiday make excellent inclusions and will also add real interest in the years to come.

FABRICS AND BRAIDS

Search in your sewing box or the local haberdasher for bits of braid, ribbon, sequin waste, embroidery threads and fabric remnants. They make wonderful additions to the pages and can be used just like any other decorative device. Alternatively, fabric or trims from a bridesmaid's gown or baby robe are ideal additions to themed albums.

PARCHMENT CRAFT

The art of parchment craft is relatively new on the hobby scene although it has a long history. Exquisite designs are created using special parchment paper (rather like tracing paper) and a few special tools. By perforating and embossing the paper, it is transformed into lace-like designs. Although painstaking, the effects are tremendously rewarding and parchment crafters themselves become addicts to this hobby.

Parchment craft pieces are well worth adding to a memory album, being itself a labour of love. If you want to know more, suppliers appear in the stockists list on page 78 and starter kits are available from the manufacturers.

COTTON PRESSES

Although the finished effect of a cotton press is quite bulky, these moulded items make ideal cover decals. They come as complete kits and produce little relief designs from cotton waste. Cotton press suppliers can be found on page 79.

ENVELOPES

Although not strictly a decorative feature, little envelopes or pockets included in your album will enable you to include keepsakes and mementoes too precious to glue onto the page. They are also ideal for really small pieces or trinkets.

Either make your own pocket from a piece of decorated paper (see Ruby Wedding Anniversary on page 54), or glue in an attractive ready-made envelope, adding a little tie from silk thread or paper string to the flap. Secure by twisting it around a button or paper tie.

EXQUISITE FEATURES A parchment craft butterfly (top) would grace any memory album cover. Flat parchment designs can be used inside. A cotton pressed motif (left) is adorned with pressed ferns and a little flower – another ideal device for album covers.

GILDED EFFECTS

You can achieve the antique effect of gilding by applying a little lustrous gilt to your album edges or covers.

The first method is to use gilt wax, sold in tubs or tubes from art shops. This metallic paste can be rubbed on to the crinkled edges of pages or any relief piece, such as a cotton press motif. The gilt picks up the highlights, creating an old-gold or bronzed effect. Perfect for a nostaglia piece.

The other way of adding gilding is to apply gold leaf. Real gold leaf is very expensive, tricky to apply and is not recommended for memory album projects. However, Dutch metal resembles the real thing and is considerably more cost effective for the user. It must be applied onto a sized surface with a soft brush and the final effect is truly sumptuous.

Try it for wooden album covers, or adorning a small item to decorate the cover.

MIDAS TOUCH Mock gold leaf, also known as Dutch metal, is sold in flimsy sheets and can be applied just like the real stuff. If you want to give your album a touch of opulence – this is what to use. Practice first as it is quite tricky to apply well.

RUBBING

For bulky items like coins, take rubbings and add these to your album. Buttons, small mouldings and medals can also be given this treatment.

Use wax or ordinary colouring crayons. Rub all over the item in the same direction using a firm stroke. When the image has appeared in full, cut off the rough edges and paste into your album.

DECOUPAGE

Another time-honoured craft that is widely used and one which offers a useful alternative to cover decoration or "title" pages of memory albums. Pictures from magazines, photocopies or prints are cut out and glued into an attractive design. The whole thing is then varnished over for protection.

Variations of the decoupage idea can be utilized for memory album enthusiasts. Try photocopying some of your favourite photographs, cutting tightly around them and "montaging" them onto a page.

HELP TO PRESERVE NUBIA'S TEMPLES
TEMPLE AND TOMBS IN DEIR EL MEDINA

THEMES

Organize your memory albums into themes. A birthday album, perhaps, with family birthdays spanning the years. Or make an album about just one particular holiday. Over the next few pages we give you some ideas to inspire you – but the choice is all yours.

OUR WEDDING

A formal wedding album is a wonderful tribute to a very special day, but a wedding memory album enables you to preserve and keep safe all the mementoes from your wedding day in one commemorative collection.

Your own memory album can include some of the "happy snaps" taken by friends and family – delightfully relaxed, informal moments that may have been missed by the official wedding photographer.

Small items which may get lost or damaged if left in a drawer can also be incorporated into your design. These could include pressed flowers, invitation and place cards, paper serviettes, a snippet of fabric from the bride's gown, confetti – anything that you have saved from the wedding that in years to come will remind you of that fantastic day.

THE WEDDING spread from a wedding memory album shows the range of other memorabilia that you can include - a piece of wedding dress fabric, pressed flowers from the bouquets, an invitation card or place setting card, some confetti. Dress up the pages with "loving" stamps - cupids, hearts, wedding rings, and cover the album in a wedding fabric. Here, we've used scraps of silk left over from the dresses of the bridesmaids. Ribbons from their dresses can be used as a page marker for the album.

TEENAGE PARTY

Like childhood, the teenage years are swiftly past, so do capture those precious (!) years on camera and make up an album or two. Teenagers will probably want to take part in compiling the album themselves, and it will provide great amusement looking back on the memories years later.

Many of us have happy memories of our own teenage parties, and now I enjoy watching my daughter and her friends have wonderful sleepovers themselves. They love pampering themselves with all the latest lotions and potions, curling their hair and painting their nails. Singing along with the latest music or watching videos seems to complete the evening.

Whether the party is to celebrate a special event, such as a birthday or perhaps the end of school exams, or for no specific reason, keeping a memory album for these occasions becomes a record of your child's teenage years and their special groups of friends.

If the party is themed or fancy-dress, your memory album could reflect this. You can use decorations from the party, menus or parts of costumes, alongside the photographs.

GIRLS JUST WANT TO HAVE FUN Capture the mood of being seventeen .... good friends, laughs, sodas and ice-cream. Stamps, stickers, lipstick kisses make for that fun-time look, and for your album ask friends to autograph the page.

PARTY POPPERS

RUBY WEDDING

This pocket-style memory album is the ideal gift to give to a happy couple who have shared 40 years worth of memories together. Store greetings cards and gift tags in the pocket to retrieve and pore over in the future.

For a ruby wedding anniversary, or indeed, any anniversary, there are small bits of commemorative ephemera that the couple may wish to keep safe, such as greeting cards and letters. A pocket page is the perfect way to store these items that may otherwise go astray or become damaged.

Cut the actual pocket from a sheet of card to the shape and size required. For a shaped pocket, like the one shown here, you could use a pair of compasses. Alternatively, simply draw around the edge of a dinner plate. Trim the edge with decorative-edged scissors and decorate the front with a punch and some small gems, or add some stickers or stamping.

Here, the colour scheme is ruby-red for this particular anniversary. You could use silver (25 years), gold (50 years), or adapt this for a wedding or engagement using white or cream.

40 WONDERFUL YEARS Get together with friends and family to gather as many small mementoes as you can to include in this album - it will make the ideal gift.

CHRISTMAS

Christmas is a special family occasion, often the one time of the year that different generations gather together. It is also a time of tradition when everyone joins in the festive customs of the season. Your memory album is a means of recording these times for future generations to come.

MERRY CHRISTMAS Touches of Victoriana add to a modern yuletide.

Christmas is such a magical time of the year, especially for small children who delight at decking the tree and switching on the lights for the first time, placing the characters in the Nativity and, of course, opening those long awaited presents. Preserve those moments year upon year in a Christmas album. The rich colours of the season really form a wonderful backdrop to your photos, and can be used as a colour scheme for your album.

Christmas is traditionally a time for crafts: making cards, gift tags, small presents and decorations for the tree. Use the seasonal touches of glossy Christmas wrapping paper, glitter, ribbon, fabric and pretty Christmas cards to make your album more interesting, both for you and the reader. Each year, you could slightly change your theme: a Victorian touch one year, a Scandinavian-style another, a 1950s retro look for another ...

EASTER

Easter always seems to be the time of year that fills us with enthusiasm. Everything is fresh and new and finally winter is over and we can begin to look forward to the warm summer months ahead.

We think of spring lambs, new leaves, buds and warmer weather. The children love the excitement of the visit from the Easter bunny, who hides small eggs in the house and garden. It is wonderful to capture on film as they excitedly run around carrying small baskets full of their found treasure.

Make a small album just celebrating one special Eastertide, or compile an album of those key holiday times, such as Easter, Christmas or New Year, when the family gathers together.

New growth in the garden is the inspiration for the handmade papers here. The flowers used in the paper can reflect the season, and look effective alongside the pressed flowers on the paper flaps.

Alternatively, you can create a more modern look by using computer generated sheets, with eggs and chicks already in place as a backdrop. Save shiny egg wrappers and include these on the page.

EASTER CHIC The spread (right) is computer generated. If you own a PC, there are various software programs available offering similar designs.

SPRINGTIME To make this album spread a little different (left), a narrow piece of paper has been added to the centre to create two paper flaps. These have been given wavy edges and pressed flower decorations. Beneath, the spread shows springtime photographs and handmade paper embedded with spring petals.

JAPANESE HOLIDAY

A trip to a faraway place is a great subject for a memory album and a chance to preserve mementoes of very different cultures. Choose or make the actual album to reflect the country that you visited.

Holidays and vacations are perfect memory-gathering occasions. Collect ephemera such as postcards, stamps, tickets, even spare banknotes to bring back home.

Here, I have selected a Japanese holiday. By purposefully excluding photographs from the collage, the culture of the country is not overshadowed by western additions or text. When using bulky items, such as the fan, use an album which has an expanding binding.

南 風
The scenic beauty of the Yaeyama islands
世界文化遺産登録
NTT

FAMILY BEACH HOLIDAY

This memory album could be typical of any traditional beach holiday. Give children sand, sea and a bucket and spade and nothing else seems to be important.

A traditional beach holiday has been enjoyed by families for many generations.

Everyone hates going home at the end of a wonderful holiday, but now you can look forward to creating a memory album of your beach holiday to cheer yourself up on gloomy, rainy days.

Take plenty of snaps. Use stamps and stickers on your pages, cream tea souvenirs or shells, pebbles and beach finds.

Where you cannot include larger shells on your page, take rubbings of them.

SAND AND SEA Here, the use of coloured and textured papers gives the effect of the sand and sea as a background for cut-out photos. It would be easy to sponge plain papers to give the same look. and you could even use sandpaper as an alternative - your own little beach back home!

AMERICAN HOLIDAY

Holidays in the United States are rarely undertaken without a trip to one of the great theme parks or movie studios – and you will have no trouble finding plenty of collectibles to add to your album.

This spread comes from a holiday album that covers a US touring holiday we enjoyed one summer. Here, we have gathered snaps and mementoes from Hollywood, the Grand Canyon and New York. To enhance the Hollywood

theme, little palm trees have been punched out of some handmade decorative paper, along with a flight of aeroplanes. Aeroplane rubber stamps also add to the holiday theme, while dollar bills, matchbooks, beer mats and maps are the collectibles chosen for this spread.
Many rubber stamp makers offer a range of holiday stamps to suit your own specific project. Here, the Statue of Liberty was the perfect addition to this page.

Mixed with jolly snapshots, the whole feature looks sunny and conjures up fond memories of a fun, although frantic, time.

MAKE A NOTE Keep a diary or a few notes when on a touring holiday. It is so easy to forget the names of places and people when making your memory album later, a note or two will remind you.

HALLOWEEN

The time for spooks, ghouls and ghostly happenings, Halloween has become a widespread favourite time of year, especially for children who love the opportunity to dress up. Plan a party, shoot some pictures and your mini-memory album is in the making.

You could entitle this memory album "Ghostly Nights" or "Nightmare on (your own address) Street". Alternatively, you could include halloween as part of an album of parties. Whatever the choice, it is a great subject and offers a host of decorative ideas.

Children find this event thrilling. Bonfire parties, firework displays and trick-or-treating can all be recorded photographically and put together with great effect to produce really colourful album pages. Crop the people and children in the photographs dramatically to achieve maximum effect against the autumnal colours of your backing paper. Include invitations to Halloween parties. If you want to use dark coloured papers, use a metallic marker to write your photo captions.

GHOSTLY GOINGS-ON Memory album and stationery suppliers provide bats and spiders, ghosts and jack o' lantern stickers and die cuts. Use orange and black backing papers and perhaps include Halloween recipes or witches' spells! However, it is the photographs that will make this album special. Insist everyone dresses up and capture your Draculas, monsters and werewolves on film. After a little spicy punch, everyone will be happy to play to your camera!

FIFTH BIRTHDAY PARTY

Year after year, birthday parties come and go. Compiling a Birthday Album will help you keep track of friends and family and will be a wonderful record in the years to come.

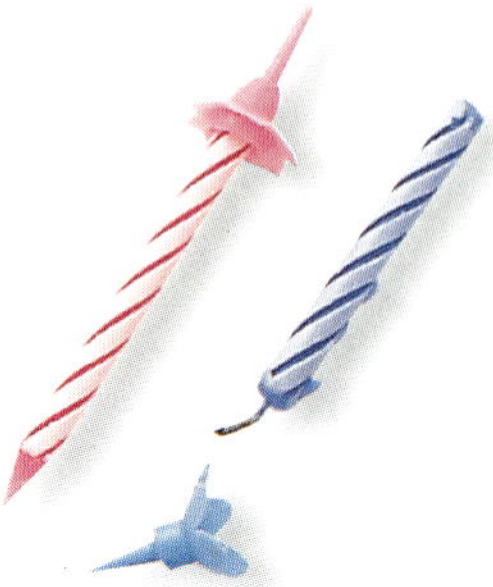

Probably one of the most photographed subjects in the world is our children. Their growth and development is always a source of constant amazement. As each birthday is a milestone: capture it and store it away in a special memory album that will provide huge pleasure many years into the future. Apart from the stickers and stamps specially designed for birthdays, don't forget to add a personal touch by recording amusing anecdotes and

asking the birthday child to write a little something about their day.

Include birthday greetings cards and remember to record names of friends attending the party. You could even ask everyone to write their names on a sheet of special paper which you can add into the album. In years to come, these will be the source of endless discussions: "Whatever happened to old Tom Connor?", for example.

HAPPY BIRTHDAY TO YOU A fifth birthday party is possibly one of the first we all remember with some sort of clarity. Children are now old enough to play games and be organised. Use bright colours or strong pastel shades (pink still seems to be a favourite with girls!) and plenty of stamps and stickers.

A BABY'S FIRST FEW MONTHS

Those first important days, weeks and months of a new baby's life are full of amazing discoveries – the first smile, first teeth and first steps. This is the chance to capture these treasured moments.

A child's development in the first six months is astounding. I think it is safe to say that we probably take more photographs of our children in the first few years than at any other time of their lives. Baby albums are therefore so precious. Try to include as many items that add to the memories of that moment in their lives. Remember, you are

not just producing this album for yourself, but to hand down to future generations. Include as much as you can to give a full picture of your baby's early development.

Photographs are obviously the key element, but add weight and health charts, birth greetings cards, hospital tags or records, snippets of first clothes, Christening mementoes and locks of hair.

Fortunately, there are plenty of stamps, stickers, stencils and other nursery paraphernalia with which to adorn your page. And don't forget to add ages or dates to the photographs, ie Katy at 3 months, 6 months, and so on, as this is the easiest thing to forget.

BEAUTIFUL BABY A new baby grows so quickly that you should try to photograph them month by month. Add ribbons, teddy and pram motifs, plus greetings cards and letters to your baby pages.

FAMILY TREE

Genealogy, the study of one's family, both past and present, has always been a very rewarding pastime. A family tree for a memory album makes the perfect subject and you will find that it soon becomes a piece of your family's history.

Most people can trace their family back to great and even great-great grandparents, so don't feel you have to dig into ancient archives to come up with ancestors. They are closer than you think! However, once you start making a family tree, you might find the whole subject totally addictive and wish to pursue your family's history in more detail. Local genealogical societies can help.

Begin by assembling old photographs. Beg from relatives – even distant ones. It might be a way of reuniting distant arms of your family. The photographs can be of people, family pets, old family homes.

As the generations go back, photographs tend to be more formal and posed, and therefore more difficult to find. You may be able to obtain an old wedding photograph which shows several generations together – this could be mounted alongside your graphical family tree.

Another source of information and pictures are old newspaper cuttings which may have been preserved. Although these are difficult to find in good condition, they often give important dates and details. Local newspapers also often print old photographs of local teams or social groups that have been sent in by readers and which could include distant relatives if you look carefully. The nearer in history you get to yourself, the more material you will find, so be selective.

If you can date the photographs, that can be of great historical value – add the names of everyone you know. Also try to provide any other information that could be relevant. For example, simply titling someone: "John Lee Jones, our grandad" has a personal note but doesn't tell any other reader of the memory album much about him. Instead, add more to the caption, making it appropriate to the picture. If John Lee Jones is in military uniform try to include what he did, where he served and anything else. So your caption could end up reading: "John Lee Jones as Captain, Light Infantry during World War I, wounded near the Somme in 1916. Grandad to Jane and Lisa Ramsey".

Rather than the traditional "tree" of lines linking the photographs, why not try using a "real" tree as your background. The tree could be hand-painted or a drawing from a book, but remember to use only acid-free inks, pens and markers. If this is to be handed down for generations to come, you need to avoid any damage or discoloration to the photographs. Faded pictures, although quite attractive, mean loss of definition and eventually the detail of faces will disappear.

As your family grows, don't move the photographs around on your tree, just start a new one. Eventually you could create a whole forest of trees!

TREE OF LIVES With photographic images of relatives carefully placed in geneological order on your tree, the whole thing comes to life. You could also incorporate much-loved family pets, family homes and other treasured memories.

L de R

GRADUATION

A proud moment for both parents and students – after years of study the reward of graduation is justly earned. Sometimes students are a little embarrassed to appear "dressed up" for photographs, but in years to come they will be pleased they did – and that you made a record of the day.

One of a few time-honoured traditions, graduation ceremonies – with all their formal dress, speeches and presentations, are an absolute must for a memory album. As the actual ceremony will be held indoors and anyone taking photographs will be far away, save your snaps

for afterwards, ouside, where you can assemble the student and groups together for informal and more posed shots.

If you follow the graduation ceremony with a special meal in a restaurant, remember to include a copy of the menu, and if you are holding a party at home, ask guests to sign a "memory" page with comments and their signatures.

This is the ideal subject for a "mini album", so why not make your own? See page 18.

OLD TRADITIONS Such a splendidly ancient ceremony needs an album that is classic and formal. Add marbled papers, thick cords, gold leaf, deckle or plain edges to create that traditional look.

W E E K E N D   A W A Y

Don't let that weekend break become a fleeting memory. Instead, preserve it. Often in just two or three days, you cram in almost as much as you can in one week. So collect menus, tickets, beer mats and place settings and create a "mini memory".

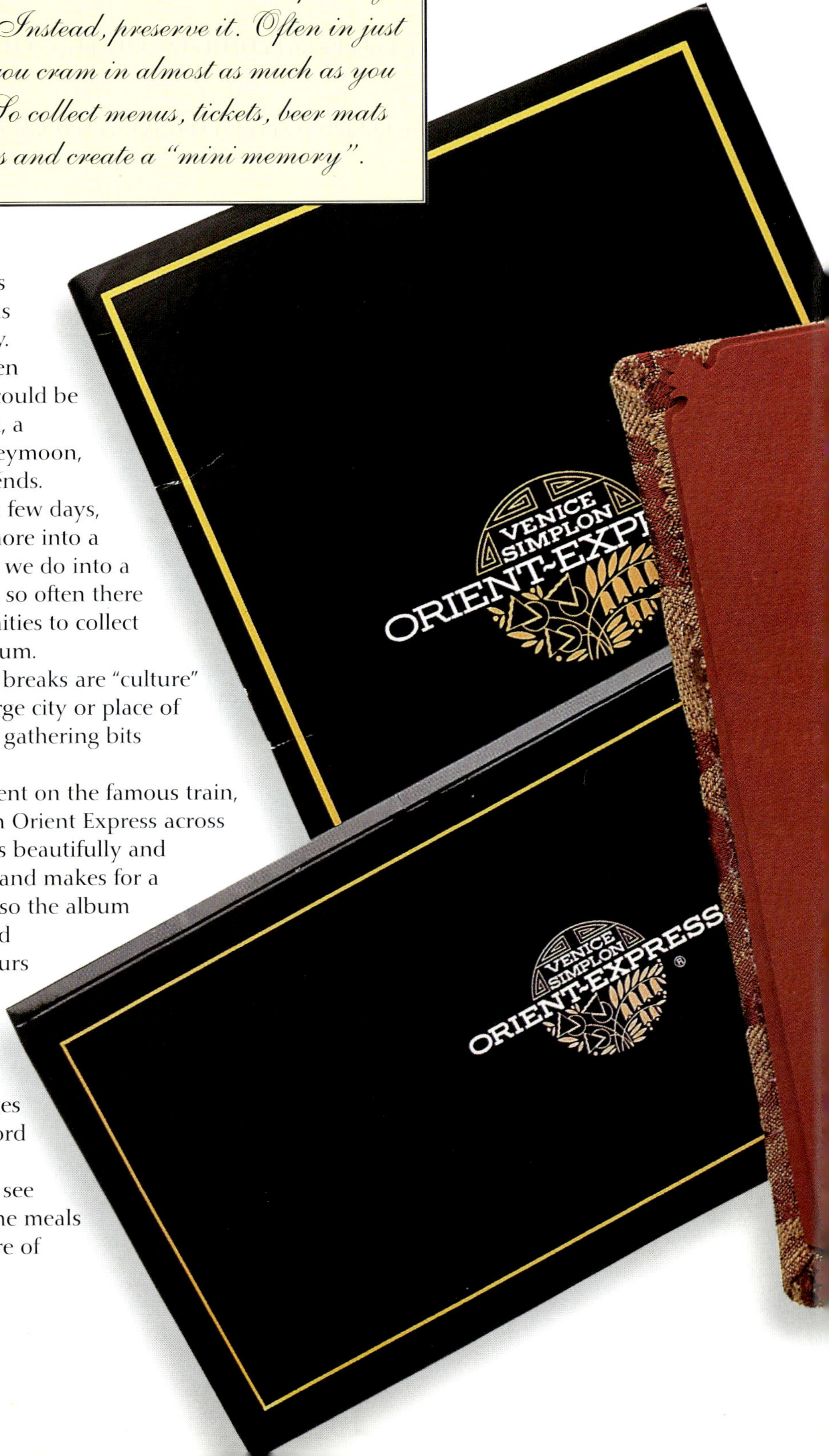

A weekend break is often more precious than a long holiday. Snatched in between work or school, it could be a romantic sojourn, a second "mini" honeymoon, or a visit to old friends. Because it is only a few days, we seem to pack more into a small holiday than we do into a long, leisurely one, so often there are more opportunities to collect things for your album.

Often weekend breaks are "culture" breaks to visit a large city or place of interest. Perfect for gathering bits of ephemera.

Here, friends went on the famous train, the Venice Simplon Orient Express across Europe. The train is beautifully and lavishly furnished and makes for a luxurious holiday, so the album was designed in old railway livery colours of deep red and green. Traditional motifs from punches appear at the tops of the pages and a thick gold cord wraps around the centre. As you can see with this spread, the meals were a main feature of the trip!

LUXURY BREAK A weekend away on the train which featured in one of Agatha Christie's most well known novels was a great treat for my friends. By collecting small tokens of their train journey and the countries they visited, my friends found they had enough to fill a small, 8 page album. Added to this were a sheaf of photographs to secure on the pages. It is a memory they will have forever preserved.

MEMORY ALBUM SUPPLIERS

UNITED KINGDOM/EUROPE

Cornelissen & Son Ltd
105 Great Russell Street
London
WC1
Tel: 0171 636 1045
Fax: 0171 636 3655
Artists materials and supplies

Craft Barn
9 East Grinstead Road
Lingfield
Surrey
RH7 6EP
Tel: 01342 836 097
Fax: 01342 835 792
Artists supplies and wooden album covers

Falkiner Fine Papers
76 Southampton Row
London
WC1B 4AR
Tel: 0171 831 1151
Fax 0171 430 1248
Specialist papers

First Class Stamps Ltd
Hall Staithe
Fakenham
Norfolk
NR21 9BR
Tel: 01328 851 449
Fax: 01328 864 828
Memory album and rubber stamp suppliers

Greene and Stone
259 Kings Road
London
SW3 5EL
Tel: 0171 352 0837
Fax: 0171 351 1098
Artists materials and drawing supplies

Kars Kreatief
Industrieweg 27
Industrieterrein 'De Heuning'
Postbus 97
4050 EB Octen
Netherlands
Memory album suppliers

Kuretake UK Ltd
10 Moon Park
Burnt Meadow Road
Redditch
Worcestershire
B98 9PA
Tel: 01527 62828
Memory album pens and markers

Paperchase
213 Tottenham Court Road
London W1A 4US
Specialist papers and craft items

Pergamano
Alcancia B.V.
Slingerduin 5
1187 EG Amstelveen
Netherlands
Parchment craft manufacturers and suppliers

Specialist Crafts Ltd
Homecrafts Direct
PO Box 38
Leicester LE1 9BU
Tel: 0116251 3139
Fax: 0116 251 5015
Wide range of art and craft items

Stone Marketing Ltd
4 Ashby's Yard
Medway Wharf Road
Tonbridge
Kent TN9 1RE
Tel: 01732 771 771
Fax: 01732 771767
Scrapbooks, albums and stationery

USA

Fiskars Inc
7811 West Stewart Avenue
Wausau
Wisconsin 54401
Tel: 715-849-2091
Fax: 715-848-3657
Stickers, stamps, papers, tools and scissors

The Gifted Line
999 Canal Boulevard
Point Richmond
CA 94804
Tel: 510-215-4777
Fax: 510-215-4772
Memory album stickers and papers

Hot Off The Press
1250 NW Third
Canby
OR 97013
Tel: 503 266-9102
Fax: 503 266-8749
Decorative papers and memory album tools

Personal Stamp Exchange
360 Sutton Place
Santa Rosa
California 95407
Tel: 707-588-8058
Fax: 707-588-74

SOUTH AFRICA

H Franken (Pty) Ltd
445 Hilda Street
Hatfield
Pretoria
Tel: (012) 362-5591
Fax: (012) 362-5600

In-Fin-Art
Shop 6135
Victoria Wharf
V&A Waterfront 8002
Cape Town
Tel: (021) 418-4008
Fax: (021) 418-4009

L&P Stationers and Art
141A Zastron Street
Bloemfontein
Tel: (051) 430-1085
Fax: (051) 430 4102

Sandton Stationery and Print
Level 4
Shop L62
Sandton City
Johannesburg
Tel: (011) 883-4462
Fax: (011) 783-0806

Story's Art and Craft
Shop 32 and 33
The Workshop
99 Aliwal Street
Durban 4001
Tel: (031) 306-1227
Fax: (031) 304-5421

AUSTRALIA

Craft Crowd, The
Shop 60 Sunnybank Plaza
Main Road, Sunnybank
Queensland 44109
Tel: (07) 345 9812

Craft Lovers
37 Murray Street
Tanunda
South Australia 5352
Tel: (08) 563 0504

Hobbytex
5 Victoria Avenue
Castle Hill NSW 2154
Tel: (02) 634 5388

Sundale Handcrafts
16B Logan Village Shopping Centre
Bryants Road
Loganholme
Queensland 4129
Tel: (07) 801 1121

NEW ZEALAND

Auckland Rubber Stamps
Unit 2, 50 Stoddard Road
Mt Roskill
Auckland
Tel: (09) 629 2692

P A Inkman Ltd
36 Douglas Stret
Ponsonby
Auckland
Tel: (09) 638 7593

INDEX